MY ENTIRE BODY BELONGS TO ME

AND I WILL ALWAYS PROTECT MYSELF!

SANDRA E. JACKSON
BESTSELLING AUTHOR OF
"RAISING CHILDREN IS NOT EASY BUT IT'S WORTH IT"

My Entire Body Belongs to Me!
Copyright @ 2025 by Dr. Sandra E. Jackson

All rights reserved. No part of this publication may be reproduced, stored in, or introduced into a retrieved system, distributed, or transmitted in any form or by any means, including photocopying, recording, or other electronic or mechanical methods, without the prior written permission of the publisher, except in the case of brief quotations embodied in critical reviews and specific other noncommercial uses permitted by copyright law.

Scanning, uploading, and distributing this book via the Internet or any other means without written permission of the visionary author, Dr. Sandra E. Jackson, is illegal and punishable by law. Please purchase only authorized electronic editions and do not participate in or encourage the electronic distribution of copyrighted material. Your support of the author's rights is appreciated.

If you have permission requests, please email the publisher at the address below, with the subject line "Attention: Permission Requests."

Library of Congress Cataloging-in-Publication Data is available upon request at 60423sandra@gmail.com

Also available in hardcover, paperback, and E-book

Library of Congress Control Number:

Printed in the United States of America

Published by Journey Into Purpose LLC.

Website: www.journeyintpurposellc.com

Email: ecstaticcoaching@gmail.com

Cover designed by www.ailadesigns.com

All research was done on the Internet.

My Entire Body Belongs to Me: And I Will Always Protect Myself!

Sandra E. Jackson,

Kindle Edition ISBN: 979-8-9927759-2-1

Paperback ISBN: 979-8-9927759-0-7

Hardcover ISBN: 979-8-9927759-1-4

"Beautiful people are not always good, but good people are always beautiful."
— *Imam Ali*

Allow this book to prepare you to enter and exit places safely!

The Author's Aim for the Book

The publication "My Entire Body Belongs to Me" is designed to empower both children and their parents by providing vital knowledge and skills about body safety.

This book underscores the significance of understanding body autonomy and children's inherent right to personal safety. It instructs children on how to identify and articulate their boundaries, distinguish between safe and unsafe touch, and confidently assert "No!" in response to unwarranted physical contact.

Furthermore, it encourages children to seek assistance and support from trusted adults, while enhancing their self-esteem by affirming the validity of their bodies and feelings.

This publication is invaluable for adolescents, parents, grandparents, caregivers, educators, educational institutions, and guardians who want to initiate and sustain open, age-appropriate dialogues about body safety. It emphasizes the importance of active listening, while fostering a safe and trustworthy environment that reassures children who disclose sensitive information.

Furthermore, it equips parents with strategies to discern potential indicators of abuse, so they can take proactive measures to prevent harm, and uphold the principle of consent throughout all stages of their child's development relationships.

Dr. Jackson seeks to foster a culture of respect and consent within families, ensuring that children and parents are prepared to discuss body autonomy confidently.

The book provides practical tools and resources to ensure

parents feel confident in helping their children understand personal safety.

Ultimately, "My Entire Body Belongs to Me" promotes a proactive rather than reactive approach to body safety by equipping families with knowledge, communication skills, and preventive strategies. The book serves as a vital resource for preventing and addressing potential sexual abuse, and fostering safer environments for children to grow and flourish.

Dr. Jackson aspires for this book to reach a wide readership, including daycare centers, nursing homes, religious institutions, libraries, youth organizations, educational institutions, sports coaches, educators, and student guardians.

Dr. Jackson hopes that this book serves as a conduit to address the pervasive issue of sexual abuse in our society.

Please do not hesitate to leave a review on Amazon and at journeyintopurposellc.com/reviews.

Warmly,

Dr. Sandra E. Jackson

Table of Contents

THE AUTHOR'S AIM FOR THE BOOK V

FOREWORD IX

CHAPTER 1 Hey, My Entire Body Belongs To Me, Not You! 19

CHAPTER 2 It Can Happen Anywhere And At Any Time 32

    You Have The Power To Say, "No!" 54

    "My Protector's Decree" 57

CHAPTER 3 Trust Your Instincts! 62

CHAPTER 4 Secrets? No Secrets Here! 65

CHAPTER 5 When? Immediately 67

CHAPTER 6 Quotes For Teenagers 70

CHAPTER 7 It's Important To Remember 75

CHAPTER 8 Affirmations About Body Safety 81

CHAPTER 9 Remember: Knowledge Allows For Open Dialogue And Authentic Conversation 83

CHAPTER 10 Remember That You Are Loved 86

CHAPTER 11   One's Body's Autonomy 90

CHAPTER 12   Teaching Parental Moments 93

CHAPTER 13   Believe That Healing Is Attainable For You! 105

ABOUT THE AUTHOR 109

DEDICATION 112

REFERENCES 113

DISCLAIMER 114

Foreword

The ability to stand confidently in one's own body is a fundamental right that should be instilled in every individual from an early age. My Entire Body Belongs to Me! It's more than just a book—it is an empowering tool designed to educate, equip, and encourage individuals to recognize their worth, establish boundaries, and protect their well-being. This book is a vital guide for children, parents, and caregivers in a world where personal safety and bodily autonomy are often challenged.

Through compassionate storytelling and clear, actionable advice, Dr. Sandra E. Jackson has created a resource that fosters awareness and open conversations about consent, boundaries, and self-protection.

This book educates and reassures children that they are never alone, and that there are trusted adults who will stand by their side.

This book is a call to action—a call to parents and educators to engage in these essential discussions, a call to children to embrace their voice, and a call to society to cultivate environments where safety, respect, and dignity are upheld. By reading and sharing this book, you are taking a stand for a future where every child feels secure, valued, and empowered. May this book serve as a beacon of knowledge, strength, and hope for all who read it.

Dr. Tamika Hall

Refined By Fire Ministries Websites:

www.tamikahall.com

http://letsgetreadytobible.com

The Pastor's Corner Endorsement: 5-Star Review

My Entire Body Belongs to Me - And I Will Always Protect Myself:

Is A Revolution of Reclamation That Must Begin Now.

Sandra E. Jackson hasn't just written a book; she's ignited a lifeline. For every teen who's felt the violation, the confusion, the crushing silence, 'My Entire Body Belongs to Me' is the answer they've desperately needed.

I boldly declare that this isn't just a dialogue; it's a deliverance. It's a raw, unflinching conversation that meets our youth in the darkest corners of their experience and pulls them into the light of truth, practical guidance, and unshakeable hope.

This book doesn't offer gentle platitudes; it delivers weapons of self-empowerment. It equips teens with the words they never knew they had, the boundaries they were told didn't exist, and the unwavering confidence to say 'NO!' with the force of their own undeniable worth.

But this isn't just for the survivors. It's for the parents who ache to understand, the pastors who yearn to heal, and the leaders who must protect. I implore us to make this book an accessible ministry resource because its pages hold the power to dismantle the atrocities that steal our children's innocence. It's a call to action, a demand for change, a declaration that 'enough is enough.

'My Entire Body Belongs to Me' is more than a book; it's a movement. It's the sound of voices rising, the shattering of silence, the reclamation of stolen power. It's the urgent, undeniable truth that everybody is sacred, every voice deserves to be heard, and every soul deserves to be protected.

Don't just read this book. Wield it. Could you share it? Demand it. Let its words become the shield and the sword for a generation that refuses to be silenced any longer. The revolution starts now, and it begins with you.

Bishop Dr. Nellie Rodgers

Healing happens between the pages, so keep reading.

Current Events:

Your safety is paramount—love yourself enough to protect it.

What Happened to a Spanish Women's Soccer Player

Jennifer Hermoso, a Spanish soccer player, was disrespected when her coach, Luis Rubiales, Spain's former top soccer official, kissed her on the mouth after they won. While she was in court before the judge, Jennifer stated, "I think it was a moment that ruined one of the happiest days of my life," referring to her team's victory in the 2023 Women's World Cup tournament.

Ms. Hermoso described her horror at the unexpected kiss from Mr. Rubiales, who is accused of sexual assault and coercion. She also testified about the distress she felt after Mr. Rubiales and other Spanish soccer leaders, waged what she called an intense campaign for her to publicly support him after the kiss ignited a social media storm. "I felt disrespected," Ms. Hermoso, 34, said in a televised testimony at the trial outside Madrid, adding, "I didn't look for that act, nor did I expect it."

A Kiss After Spain's World Cup Win Prompts Many to Cry Foul (Published 2023). A Soccer Federation chief kissed the Spanish forward Jennifer Hermoso fully on the lips during the medal's ceremony, an unpleasant reminder to many of the sexism plaguing women's soccer.

What Happened to a School-Aged Student in Kenosha

A former elementary school staffer already accused by Wisconsin authorities of sexually assaulting a child is facing additional criminal charges after investigators identified more alleged victims.

Anna-Marie Crocker, 33, is charged in an amended criminal complaint filed on Nov. 1 in Kenosha County Circuit

Court with exposing genitals, exposing a child to harmful material, child enticement, and exposing a child to harmful descriptions, as per the Kenosha County District Attorney's Office. The charges came less than a month after Crocker, who worked at Riverview Elementary School in Silver Lake, Wis., was charged with first-degree child sexual assault, or having sexual intercourse with a child under age 13. She was also charged with possession of child pornography, and sexual exploitation of a child, or filming, according to the initial criminal complaint filed on Oct. 14 in Kenosha County Circuit Court and shared by prosecutors.

It is unclear if Crocker has entered pleas, and PEOPLE couldn't immediately identify an attorney who could speak on her behalf. **Jail records** show she is being held on a $500,000 bond.

The alleged victims related to Crocker's initial case were current and former students at the elementary school, the Kenosha County Sheriff's Department **said in a statement** last month. Authorities added that the alleged misconduct did not occur during school hours or on school property.

According to the criminal complaint, a sheriff's deputy was called to a home in Twin Lakes, Wis., on Oct. 8, where the caller claimed his 13-year-old son was "forced to have sex with the mother of his friend." The 13-year-old alleged the sexual assault happened in the wintertime, when he was at Crocker's house for a sleepover with some friends, as per the complaint. The boy claimed he was asleep on the couch in the basement when Crocker, who was naked, woke him up and removed his pants before sexually assaulting him, the complaint stated.

What Happened to an Ohio Infant at a Daycare Facility

Conner Walker, a 21-year-old from Rocky River, Ohio, was sentenced to 35 years in prison for sexually assaulting a toddler at an in-home daycare and distributing footage of this horrific abuse. Walker, who had access to the daycare through his friendship with the owner's son, admitted to the crimes in August and pleaded guilty to multiple charges, including sexual exploitation of children, attempted exploitation of children, receipt and distribution of child pornography, and possession of child pornography. US District Court Judge Bridget Meehan Brennan, who handed down the sentence on Wednesday, described Walker's actions as "horrifying" and ordered him to pay $75,000 in restitution.

Federal investigators uncovered Walker's crimes in January 2024 after a "reliable foreign partner" alerted them of disturbing child sexual abuse material (CSAM), authorities said. The images depicted a toddler, whose appearance closely matched that of a Cleveland-based child seen in family photos on Facebook, as reported by WKYC.

The FBI contacted the child's mother, who identified their 2-year-old daughter as the victim. She also noted that the hand in the images had a lighter complexion and provided investigators with the names of white men who had access to the children at the daycare.

FBI agents visited Tonya Ball's Parma Heights daycare. Ball told investigators that two adult men were at the home at the time. One was Walker, her son's friend who frequently slept over.

During the investigation, Walker admitted that one evening in fall 2023, the toddler wandered into the bathroom as he got out of the shower. He then instructed her to open her mouth before assaulting her and recorded the attack for approximately two minutes, according to court records as per WKYC. Walker shared the grotesque footage in a group chat via an encrypted messaging app called "Session." Investigators discovered that Walker was involved in many "Session" chats that distributed CSAM.

"Our lives begin to end the day we become silent about things that matter."
— Dr Martin Luther king Jr

"Don't be ashamed of your story—it will inspire others."
— Anonymous

"I can be changed by what happened to me, but I refuse to be reduced by it."
— Maya Angelou

"You're not a victim for sharing your story. You are a survivor setting the world on fire with your truth. And you never know who needs your light, warmth, and courage."
— Alex Elle

CHAPTER 1

Hey, My Entire Body Belongs to Me, Not You!

Everyone deserves safety and protection, as it is a fundamental human right. However, safety is not confined to physical aspects but also encompasses emotional, spiritual, mental, and digital dimensions. It's about being empowered to navigate your world without feeling vulnerable or unsettled.

When you recognize your strengths, values, and self-worth, living in fear becomes impossible. Therefore, setting concrete boundaries, assertively saying "No!" and commanding respect from others are essential skills that will prepare you for the real world.

However, to accomplish this, you must have a keen awareness, which means you must be present and fully conscious of your surroundings, regardless of the location. Additionally, having confidence in yourself and your capability to handle any situation is essential, as you are your best advocate.

Lastly, action is a powerful tool. One should be prepared to take proactive steps, such as understanding your triggers, attending self-defense classes, strengthening your support network, and researching ways to prevent developing a passive personality. Timidity can be a significant flaw, so it's wise to deepen one's understanding of assertiveness by recognizing when passivity occurs.

One of the greatest gifts you can offer yourself is developing a sustainable mental mindset, as this is essential for maintaining your sanity. When you finish reading this book, you will possess certain skills that last a lifetime. Please repeat this sentence: "My body is extraordinary and deserves complete wellness 24/7. Therefore, I will always ensure my safety."

Taking proper care of your body means protecting yourself from hurt, harm, and danger from any direction. It should be an automatic response to anyone who approaches you that triggers discomfort. Just as you blink your eyes, brush your teeth, and wash your face and hands, you must recognize how essential it is to keep your body safe around the clock. You have the power within to protect yourself.

For many, body autonomy is a challenging topic; however, we can't afford to whisper or avoid it any longer. It's time to engage in essential dialogue to empower and educate teenagers and parents about what to do, what not to do, and when and where to do it. Here are some helpful tips to keep yourself safe: First, recognize that your personal space belongs entirely to you without apologizing.

No one has the right to touch you in a way that makes you feel unsafe, uncomfortable, or uneasy. Always remember, your body belongs to you, and you alone.

For example: your aunt, uncle, niece, nephew, mother, father, sister, brother, grandma, grandpa, teacher, coach, boss, priest, deacon, pastor, employee, family friend, daycare provider, and those with access to the daycare, or any other person does not have permission to invade your personal space.

Will you allow me to help you build self-confidence and awareness? The first step is learning to assert yourself with authority. Begin today by practicing in the mirror and saying firmly, "No!" It's better to be prepared and never need it than to be caught off-guard and wish you were ready. I trust you to start building your strength today—let's start right now!

Work Hard to Maintain Each Child's Innocence!

I want you to say this at least five times daily: "(Your Name), I love you, adore you, and cherish you. I will protect you 24/7. I will always do what is right, regardless of who else is involved. I will never allow anyone to hurt me physically, emotionally, financially, spiritually, mentally, or psychologically. I will protect myself unapologetically."

Next, what should you do if you feel uncomfortable? No matter where you are, you must remain safe. Whether in the bathtub, in bed, at camp, on the school bus, at the playground, or riding to the grocery store. If you believe someone's touch is wrong, you must act on it immediately. I recommend talking to a trusted person or adult. In the event someone violates your personal space, it is imperative to report them; refrain from protecting or covering for those involved, as such actions will undermine your integrity. Reading further will uncover essential and valuable information regarding your necessary next steps.

Depending on the location of this incident, you must report it using the established procedures. It is crucial to recognize that time is of the essence; the situation requires immediate attention. You should seek assistance from a helpline or trusted adult. Post-violation isn't the time to return home, isolate yourself, and succumb to feelings of depression, sorrow, blame, grief, and profound sadness. The urgency of reporting early is to keep all evidence fresh and ensure you will not forget any details.

How quickly must you act? Immediately! Urgently!
As if it is a life-or-death situation. When? Quickly, right NOW!

The Reporting Process: Understand who to report to.

- Your safety is the top priority! If you're experiencing abuse and are in imminent danger, find a safe place quickly.

♦ There are anonymous hotlines for victims and their parents listed later in this book. Having someone who is unknown is cathartic.

♦ If you have injuries or health concerns related to transmittable diseases, seek medical assistance; they can help. Remember to document the incident properly.

♦ Law enforcement can be an excellent choice because of their capability to investigate and file a criminal report that works to your advantage.

♦ Find a trained spokesperson to advocate for you, like an attorney representing your best interests.

♦ For incidents on university or school grounds, seek out Campus Security, Title IX coordinators, or school officials.

♦ For workplace incidents, seek out your Human Resources department or a supervisor.

♦ For incidents within a religious setting, seek out your pastor, organizing coordinator, a hotline, or a help department. (800-656-HOPE)

Will you have the emotional readiness to share personal details with strangers? Not really; betrayal and sexual assault can be emotionally devastating. However, do not let internal or external pressures influence you because there is no right or wrong way to handle abuse. How will you start the reporting process? Just say it! For example: "Mom/Dad, my brother, sister, coach, doctor, uncle, aunt, teacher, pastor, bus driver, or peer disrespectfully touched my private parts. I was in the bathroom when…" Describe the details. Write down the time, location, and any information on the incident that you can remember—immediately.

Why is this important? When trauma occurs, you might overlook critical details. These specifics are essential for pressing charges and achieving success in court. Remember that confidentiality laws prevent agencies and authorities from violating your privacy; trust the process.

However, you aren't required to share your experiences if you don't want to. Regardless, you will need a supportive network, whether it's a therapist, a pastor, a coach, a mentor, close friends, or your parents.

INNOCENCE

It is the quality of having no experience or knowledge of life's more complex or unpleasant aspects—naivete, simplicity, inexperience, freshness, blamelessness, righteousness, clean hands, and uprightness. Child, protect your innocence at any cost. Parents, your children are innocent; defend them at any cost.

The person who experienced abuse is not at fault! Trust your feelings. If something feels wrong, it probably is. It is okay to say "NO!" and walk away.

- Believe in yourself. (Self-validation is key.)
- Do not second-guess your decisions.
- Your feelings are valid.
- Your body is valuable.
- Your space is important.
- You have the right to protect yourself.
- You owe it to yourself to ensure your safety.
- Most perpetrators are not easily identifiable; they do not have a specific appearance.
- Your body belongs to you; you can say yes or no without needing to explain.
- Be strong, bold, and unapologetic in your choices.
- You have a future to safeguard.
- Never let anyone talk you out of your initial decision.
- Stand firm and leave any unsafe situation.
- You might need to say no over the phone, so be ready.
- Recognize when someone starts crossing boundaries.
- You possess the strength to protect yourself; do not be afraid.
- If you're scared, proceed anyway.
- Parents and children should keep their clothes on and

never be undressed around others.

♦ Dress appropriately for your age; being age-appropriate in clothing can help prevent abuse.

Your safety is achievable!

What are acceptable and unacceptable touches?

Good touches always make you feel happy and safe. For example, when a parent sees their child, young or old, they automatically embrace each other. Natural hugs from your parents are therefore considered appropriate. Additionally, giving a high-five to a friend is acceptable. Finally, patting family and friends for their accomplishments, support, and encouragement is also considered a good touch.

"It is a proven fact that good physical touches release endorphins

in your body, strengthen relationships, and boost well-being. Good touches are necessary. The effects of oxytocin extend beyond just emotional responses. It contributes to the strengthening of social bonds and relationships. Research has shown that physical touch activities, such as group singing or high-intensity martial arts training, can increase participants' oxytocin levels. This hormone helps cement the relationships vital to psychological health."

— *Our mental health.*

When a person embraces you, ensure the interaction remains pure and comfortable. If there is any other action, you must resist it immediately.

So, suppose a parent, guardian, coach, family member, teacher, daycare provider, anyone connected to the daycare center, a friend on the playground, or someone in a quiet or isolated place runs up to you and tries to hug you from the back, touching or caressing your private parts, in that case, you must take a quick stand.

Speaking up right away is necessary! Hugs are generally all right from the front if they are not invading your personal space and body parts!

If you feel paralyzed, speechless, or unable to speak verbally, you must quickly move yourself or the person out of the way. This personality trait is called assertiveness. To have assertive behavior, you must not be fearful. Fear has torment; it blocks the ability to act or react at the proper time. Being afraid of adults because they are older, taller, more prominent, or appear to be a threat can cause an innocent person to become a victim.

Be fearless, assertive, confident, and brave, and display self-empowerment! Once you are safe, you can process the other unbelievable emotions that may take over your body.

"Oxytocin as the 'Cuddle Hormone.' Oxytocin's reputation as the 'cuddle hormone' stems from its role in promoting physical and emotional intimacy. Oxytocin levels increase during skin-to-skin contact, fostering a sense of connection and comfort.

This mainly affects mothers and infants, enhancing bonding and attachment.

In romantic partnerships, oxytocin surges during intimate moments, intensifying feelings of love and affection. It contributes to the emotional satisfaction derived from physical touch and closeness.

Oxytocin's effects extend beyond romantic relationships. It can be released during social interactions, group activities, and even when petting animals, promoting feelings of trust and social bonding.

Touch is a complex sensory experience involving specialized receptors in the skin and neural pathways to the brain.

Physical contact stimulates these receptors, triggering various physiological and psychological responses." —Our Mental Health.

Healing happens between the pages, so keep reading.

My Entire Body Belongs to Me! And I Will Always Protect Myself!

You have the power inside of you to protect yourselves.

Have you ever felt like the little girl in the photo? This look is the uncomfortable look I am trying to prevent by providing a step-by-step guide throughout each chapter.

She is disheveled. Her life as she once knew it is gone forever because her innocence has been stolen. Why? An unsolicited person crossed personal boundaries and violated her privacy and body parts. I want to use examples to heighten your awareness that not everyone who looks innocent or respectful is.

Revealing timidity can be dangerous! Showing shyness to a perpetrator can mean you are vulnerable, which could lead to you becoming their prey.

Example: Many pet-lovers enjoy having snakes; they bring them home as pets, handle them, interact with them daily, and feed them. However, dangerous and poisonous snakes should never be played with. They are meant to stay in the wild. When my children were young, I taught them an unforgettable rhyme about how to watch out for dangerous snakes.

"Red or yellow, kill a fellow; red on black, venom lack."

Learning who you can communicate with and who is off-limits at an early age is imperative. Be alert and aware 24 hours a day, 365 days a year, including spring, summer, fall, and winter.

While creating a safe environment, remember that your sense of security can be deceptive, even within your home where everyone is to be trusted. However, your home may be where you need to heighten your awareness. No one is off limits to be trusted full-time. Stay alert! This knowledge is crucial for the early detection of potential threats. Conversely, your school may not be a safe place either; data on sexual assaults and abuse committed by teachers, principals, deans, and coaches are available on the Internet.

We tend to trust our synagogues, churches, pastors, school officials, and leaders of all ages.

However, the statistics on sexual abuse are shocking, as not everyone involved in church, coaching, teaching, or watching our children has pure intentions or is free from wrongdoing.

Safety rules must be implemented before your children and family arrive.

What constitutes a healthy relationship? Consent refers to the permission given for something to occur or the agreement to engage in an activity. It signifies allowing something to happen, essentially meaning to agree or approve in a mutual understanding among two or more individuals. According to Webster's Dictionary, consent encompasses the willingness or emotions involved and indicates compliance with what is proposed or wished for.

(https://www.merriam-webster.com/dictionary/consent).

Silence and passivity do not signify consent! Furthermore, online communication can lure and entrap you into engaging with a predator. Only use these platforms with safety apps, such as parental controls, which can establish boundaries for our safety.

Parents should not assume their children inherently know how to respond or communicate. When they notice warning signs or red flags, including grooming, manipulation, or boundary violations, educating them about potential dangers is essential. The instructions must come from their parents, whom they trust.

Since anyone is capable of victimizing you, stay vigilant!

CHAPTER 2

It Can Happen Anywhere and at Any Time

I have heard many personal stories of people visiting someone's home while their parents were away. Although it started as friends communicating, playing, and getting something to eat, it somehow turned into someone's life being forever altered for the worse. Or what about going into the bathroom at school to relieve yourself and finding a bully in there forcing people to do things that they never dreamed of?

Innocent people have ridden on public transportation, the bus, or on a local mode of transportation, and the driver slipped his hands under their clothing or violated them before dropping them off at their homes or places of business.

Look at the Catholic Church, which faces continuous accusations of abuse involving altar servers. Many court cases have been settled, and a few priests have been sentenced to jail-time because, year in and year out, as the altar servers went to church innocently for service to God, it turned into indescribable violent sexual acts.

Here is a *Los Angeles Times* article by Richard Winton and Hannah Fry, published October 16th, 2024.

- "L.A. Catholic Church payouts for clergy abuse top $1.5 billion with new record settlement The Archdiocese of Los Angeles had previously paid $740 million to victims in various settlements, bringing the total payout to over $1.5 billion.

- Archdiocesan officials have said the Church has made great strides to prevent abuse.

- More than 300 priests who worked in the archdiocese in Los Angeles have been accused in public records of sexually abusing minors.

"In what could be the closing chapter in a landmark legal battle, the Archdiocese of Los Angeles has agreed to pay $880 million to victims of clergy sexual abuse dating back decades in the largest settlement involving the Catholic Church.

Attorneys for 1,353 people who allege that they suffered horrific abuse at the hands of local Catholic priests settled after months of negotiations with the archdiocese. The agreement caps a quarter-century of litigation against the most populous archdiocese in the United States.

Attorneys for the victims say the settlement leaves only a few lawsuits pending against the church in Los Angeles."

My Entire Body Belongs to Me! And I Will Always Protect Myself!

Be on your guard whether jogging, walking, or going to the bus.

Can you recall the many stories of women and children walking to their bus stops or jogging to stay healthy, only to be attacked by strangers who sexually assaulted, abused, or even murdered them? If we took the time to consider the numerous movies centered around sexual abuse and rapes, whether fictional or based on actual events, we would likely take a stronger stand for victims.

From their perspective, we can inquire about what support would look like and assist them meaningfully. Let's do more than listen to and witness their pain. Today, we can commit to partnering with or advocating for the victims on a larger scale.

We trust our coaches and teachers with our children every day, as we should be able to. However, watching the news and seeing the many victims from state to state and across the country is embarrassing.

Did you hear about the 22-year-old jogger who was sexually assaulted while running on a trail in Florida? Here's an excerpt from the article for you to read.

"A 22-year-old jogger was attacked and sexually assaulted while she was running on a Florida trail Monday night—just weeks after Tennessee mother Eliza Fletcher was kidnapped and murdered by a stranger while out for a run. The young woman was jogging in Wekiwa Springs near West Wekiva Trail and Harrogate Place around 8:40 p.m. on Monday when 19-year-old Mr. William Paul Stamper allegedly approached her from behind and knocked her to the ground, police said.

"'He was moving his body in a sexual motion. She had indicated that he was aroused,' Seminole County Sheriff Dennis Lemma told WESH. After Stamper had tossed the woman to the ground, she screamed, 'Who are you? Get off of me!' according to the arrest report obtained by the outlet. Stamper coldly told her to 'shut the [expletive] up, [expletive],' in response, the report says. A person nearby heard the two struggling, and the victim told them to call 911, police said."

Things the Perpetrator Wants You to Do to Which You Should Do the Opposite.

- They say to remain silent, but you should scream for help and cry out loudly! NO! Or STOP! Don't do that! If you touch me, I will press charges!
- They say not to fight back or resist! Instead, you should empower yourself to bite, scratch, kick, punch, or use something nearby to distract them.

- They say not to tell anyone! They rely on you to keep everything a secret for life. You should disagree and inform the authorities!

- They want you to return for more, so they leave a lasting impression of fear, making it easier to repeat the cycle. Don't let them trap you with fear tactics. At this time, you should not show fear!

- They want you to return for more: You should resist unapologetically, knowing the cycle will continue without proper intervention.

- Most importantly, most predators have been victimized, and they need help! You should report them immediately.

Silence is not acceptable!

I empower you to speak UP!

Parents and children must recognize that their closest friends and associates are not exempt from scrutiny simply because of their relationships. Each interaction or visit necessitates due diligence and assessment. Given that numerous inappropriate encounters involving family members, friends, friends of friends, and acquaintances may occur within the household, parents need to exercise discernment and maintain heightened awareness.

Setting and enforcing rules may not be easy, but it is ultimately beneficial and can prevent a life of sorrow.

Maintaining vigilance may necessitate leaving the child's door ajar or conducting periodic inspections throughout the residence to ascertain ongoing activities and identify visitors. Additionally, you must establish boundaries and regulations when extending invitations to individuals into one's home, which is considered a personal sanctuary.

Children possess an inherent capacity for trust that requires guidance toward appropriate discernment. It is essential to acknowledge that not all individuals are trustworthy; therefore, trust must be cultivated over time rather than afforded unconditionally.

My parents installed a security alarm system throughout our residence. At a designated time, my father would inspect the premises and inform all occupants that they were not permitted to leave their respective rooms once the alarm was activated.

While guests were present, he took the necessary precautions to ensure their safety by advising them to stay in their rooms until morning, when the alarm would be deactivated. Each room has an adjoining bathroom, eliminating the need for guests to leave their accommodations. As responsible guardians, we must commit ourselves to enhancing our efforts to protect everyone on the premises.

Rules for Preventative Measures

a) Should you require the use of restroom facilities, please proceed in pairs, as this buddy system serves as a preventative measure.

b) It is advisable to sit with your family to avoid any uncertainty regarding the whereabouts of each member.

c) When attending a meeting, ensure that you remain in the presence of a group and do not become isolated.

d) If you are asked to undertake a task, please seek permission from your parents before departing.

e) If the intention is to go outside, one mustn't exit unaccompanied.

f) When visiting the library, it is essential to ensure that a trustworthy individual accompanies you.

g) If an individual informs you that your parents have authorized them to transport you to a particular location, you must consult with your parents before consenting to accompany them.

h) Never enter any vehicle without the explicit permission of your parents.

i) Should someone request that you ride with them, it is imperative that you assertively decline by stating, "NO!"

j) Prioritize your safety and maintain distance from individuals who do not qualify as trustworthy family members.

Keep in mind that your safety is essential!

a) It is imperative to avoid venturing into dark and isolated locations, irrespective of who may request your presence there.

b)   Always ensure that you identify an exit-strategy from any given area.

c)   If you experience discomfort, trusting your instincts and vacating the situation is crucial.

d)   It is essential to acknowledge that any individual may potentially be a perpetrator.

The repercussions of abuse can be profound and lasting. Access to the bedroom is strictly restricted to the individual currently occupying it, which is you. Never allow anyone to lure you with ice cream, candy, employment, personal goods, or money.

e)   One should never assume personal safety; ensuring that one is indeed safe is imperative.

f)   It is advisable to keep one's mobile phone switched on at all times. Maintaining a continuous location service on one's phone is likewise recommended.

g)   Furthermore, it is crucial to avoid obstructing authorities, even in situations of disagreement. Maintaining a clear state of mind is essential.

h)   Avoid listening to loud music in public through earphones, iPods, or similar devices. It is unadvisable to visit the park unaccompanied.

i)   Always inform someone of your whereabouts.

j)   If your parents are unaware of your location, they may be unable to assist you in an emergency.

k)   Should you find yourself in a vehicle and feel unsafe, it is crucial to leave evidence.

l) In dangerous situations, communicate discreetly; consider texting someone or dialing 911.

m) Honesty regarding your companions and your destination is always paramount.

n) Your plans may ultimately become a matter of critical importance pertaining to life or death.

o) Know that you are loved by a community, not just one or two people.

Children: Safety Measures Are Necessary

Your parents are not displaying excessive protectiveness by inquiring about your whereabouts, companions, and the duration of your activities. Their concern stems from a place of love, underscoring their desire for your safety and well-being until your return home.

We recognize your wish to demonstrate independence and appreciate your efforts in transitioning to adulthood. Nevertheless, it is advisable to consistently inform someone of your whereabouts, as this is fundamental for your safety.

Even if a camera is not in sight, use your eyes to see potential trouble.

Effects of Abuse
There Are Treatment Options

A. Post-Traumatic Stress Disorder stems from various types of abuse.

B. Forgetting Personal life details

C. Trust issues

D. Anxiety

E. Depression

F. Eating disorders

G. Emotional distress

H. Low Self-Esteem

I. Extreme nervousness

J. Substance Abuse

K. Numbing Mechanisms:

L. Medical Issues: Asthma, allergies, ulcers, etc.

STATISTICS: Abuse in School

How significant is this issue? One in three teens experience some form of abuse, which means that 33% of any student population is affected. Out of 1,000 students, 333 will have a horror story related to abuse. Although the education system has existed since the 17th century, no definitive protective measures have been established. Nevertheless, adolescents must be equipped with the necessary tools to safeguard themselves without exception.

Furthermore, parents must know how to navigate potential situations that may arise effectively and protectively.

There has been a lack of training for principals, faculty, teachers, and staff regarding issues such as substance abuse, anxiety, isolation, absenteeism, depression, eating disorders, and failing academics.

Out of 1000 students, 333 of them will have a horror story of abuse.

"Although sexual abuse is a widespread, known problem, not much is done to prevent it. Therefore, allow this guide to steer you in the right direction. At home, school, and work, 10% of all teens in school have reported sexual violence from a dating partner within the last year, according to RAINN. Child Protective Services stands by the fact that every 9 minutes they substantiate or find evidence for a claim of child sexual abuse."

Statistics: Rape is a Thing

1. Report a rape immediately.

2. Avoid showering until after a rape kit has been collected.

3. Of every 1,000 assaults, around 310 are reported to authorities.

4. One in 9 girls and 1 in 20 boys under the age of 18 experience abuse or assault.

5. 82% of all victims are under 18 and are primarily female.

6. Females aged 16-19 are 4 times more likely than the general population to be victims of rape, attempted rape, or sexual assault.

The Effects of Child Sexual Abuse

1. Long-term impact on physical health.

2. Mental Health Issues.

3. 4 times more likely to develop a system of drug abuse.

4. 4 times more likely to experience PTSD (post-traumatic stress disorder) as an adult.

5. 4 times more likely to experience a major depressive episode as an adult.

6. Eating disorder.

7. Obesity.

8. Relational issues.

9. Socioeconomic outcomes.

10. Outbursts.

11. Borderline emotional and personal disorders.

12. Withdrawn.

13. Poor Hygiene.

14. Overstimulation.
15. Mind never stops.
16. Difficulty sleeping through the night.
17. Wetting the bed.
18. Verbal disadvantage.

Stunning Statistics

According to RAINN:

93% of all victims know their perpetrators.

7% are strangers.

59% are acquaintances.

34% are family members.

The National Sexual Assault Hotline | 800-656-HOPE |
Website: Online.rainn.org

Visit: rainn.org/statistics/children-and-teens

Recommended book: Are You Ok? By Kati Morton

Soothing song: Oh, the Deep, Deep Love of Jesus

Quote: "Safety is a belt you should never unbuckle." ~unknown

Quote: "Safety isn't expensive; it's priceless." ~Jerry Smith

Psychosocial Impacts

Inappropriate physical contact can significantly disrupt hormonal regulation, emotional stability, and personal identity. It may lead individuals to reassess their previous understandings of the world, causing them to withdraw and construct a distorted sense of reality. Furthermore, due to confusion surrounding the events and their reasons, individuals may attempt to conceal their distress from their loved ones.

*Researchers have also **documented** many negative social consequences of CSA, including:*

- *Relationship disruption (break-up/**divorce**)*
- *Dissatisfaction with their relationships*
- *Sexual unfaithfulness/promiscuity*
- *Increased sexual dysfunction*

*"Sadly, there is considerable evidence to suggest that those who have experienced CSA are also likely to be revictimized. A **recent study** involving 12,252 survivors found that 47.5% were sexually victimized again later in life. Similarly, there is also **evidence to suggest** that the children of women who have been abused are also more likely to be abused themselves, indicating that the cycle of abuse may continue into the next generation."*

(Psychology Today)

What are the next steps in your journey? Your once-vibrant and outgoing personality has diminished, and you no longer embody the innocence, optimism, fulfillment, and trust that characterized your previous self. Your life appears to have taken a negative turn, leaving you frightened, vulnerable, and wary of others. Consequently, you find yourself perplexed by the actions and behaviors of those around you, leading you to question the intentions of all individuals. Since you know inappropriate physical interactions evoke fear, confusion, and discomfort, leaving one in a daze, merely existing but not living life to the full, I urge you to protect yourself.

The Elderly and Individuals with Disabilities Are Targets of Abuse

April is designated as Sexual Assault Awareness Month, a time during which we recognize that sexual abuse has emerged as a global epidemic. Individuals with disabilities, including children and adults, are particularly vulnerable and have regrettably become prime targets for perpetrators.

Consequently, it is imperative to maintain vigilance and impart essential lessons to empower these individuals to protect themselves, as they are 3 times more likely to experience sexual assault.

Since the elderly are already at a disadvantage, experiencing sexual abuse further deteriorates their mental health, potentially resulting in long-term effects such as loneliness, going mute, uncontrollable emotional outbursts, anxiety, depression, deep sadness, and even an increased likelihood of perpetuating abuse themselves. However, there are resources available.

Elderly support is accessible through the Yellow Pages or online. It offers support to individuals and families who are disabled, disadvantaged, or in need.

Visible warning signs to look out for are sudden shifts in behavior, such as a usually cheerful person unexpectedly becoming withdrawn, and posture changes, such as walking with their head down, crying easily, or appearing distant. Such changes should prompt thorough conversations, deeper concerns, and actions.

It is sad to say that over 70% of disabled individuals have experienced abuse. However, with age, many may not fully understand the difference between appropriate and inappropriate touch or recognize when boundaries have been violated. It is our responsibility to be their advocates, to remain observant, and to take preemptive steps to protect them.

This issue can no longer be overlooked or ignored. Safety measures should be implemented wherever they are, such as buses, facilities, restrooms, and all modes of transportation.

The elderly often experience a diminished sense of independence and rely on their families, friends, and care facilities for assistance with essential daily activities such as bathing, feeding, dressing, and managing social interactions.

They constitute the community that has nurtured and supported us; thus, we must reciprocate by providing them with enhanced care and support.

There is a call to unite in our efforts to significantly improve the lives of older people. They have made valuable contributions to society—the elderly merit superior care. By changing our perceptions of them, we can ensure their placement in higher-quality care facilities staffed by individuals who genuinely value and recognize their contributions to our communities.

The Importance of Community for Older Adults: A Key to Healthy Aging

"As a Gerontologist specializing in aging in place, the considerable debate question is always how to keep those individuals who want to remain at home engaged and part of a community. This was especially challenging during the COVID-19 pandemic when it became more difficult to connect in person and the impact of social isolation took center stage. It is essential for our organization to promote community and social connections among our members because of the health benefits associated with this type of engagement. There are many ways we can help people remain connected.

While physical health is often emphasized as we grow older, the role of the community in promoting emotional well-being, cognitive function, and overall life satisfaction is equally crucial. This is also why we have partnered with organizations like Edenwald that will offer our members opportunities to participate in a larger community. We also strive to conduct periodic member social and educational events throughout the year."

"Loneliness and social isolation are common issues among older adults, particularly those living alone or experiencing mobility challenges. Research has shown that social isolation can lead to a range of adverse health outcomes, including depression, anxiety, and even cognitive decline. Being part of a community provides regular opportunities for social interaction, which can significantly improve mental health and reduce feelings of loneliness." (Wesley)

Engaging with others helps keep the mind active and stimulated. Conversations, shared activities, and casual social interactions can challenge the brain and improve cognitive function. This mental engagement is vital in preventing or delaying the onset of conditions like dementia and Alzheimer's disease. A strong sense of community offers emotional support, which becomes increasingly important as people age. Older adults often face life transitions, such as retirement, the loss of a spouse, or changes in physical abilities.

A supportive community can provide the encouragement and understanding needed to navigate these changes. A community also fosters a sense of belonging, essential for emotional well-being. Feeling connected to others and knowing that you are part of a group where you are valued and understood can enhance self-esteem and overall happiness.

Community involvement can also positively impact physical health. Many communities offer group exercise classes, walking clubs, and other fitness activities for older adults. Participating in these activities promotes physical health and provides a social outlet, making exercise more enjoyable and sustainable.

Furthermore, being part of a community often means accessing resources and information that can help older adults manage their health. For instance, community centers may offer health screenings, educational workshops, and support groups that address various aspects of aging, from nutrition to chronic disease management.

Opportunities for Purpose and Contribution

One of the most profound benefits of being part of a community is the opportunity to contribute and find purpose. Many older adults find fulfillment in volunteering, mentoring, or participating in community projects. These activities provide a sense of purpose and accomplishment, key components of healthy aging. Community contributions also allow older adults to pass on their knowledge, skills, and life experiences to younger generations, fostering intergenerational connections and mutual respect.

Building and Maintaining Community

Given the importance of community for older adults, it's essential to take steps to build and maintain these connections. Here are some ways to foster a sense of community:

1. ***Join Local Groups:*** *Many communities have clubs, social groups, and organizations that cater to older adults. Whether it's a book club, gardening group, or senior center activities, joining these groups can provide regular social interaction.*

2. ***Volunteer:*** *Volunteering is a great way to meet new people, stay active, and contribute to the community. Many organizations actively seek older volunteers for their experience and reliability.*

3. ***Stay Connected with Family and Friends:*** *Regular communication with family and friends, whether through phone calls, video chats, or in-person visits, is crucial. These relationships provide emotional support and a sense of belonging.*

4. ***Embrace Technology:*** *While face-to-face interactions are irreplaceable, technology can help bridge the gap when physical meetings aren't possible. Social media, online forums, and video calls can keep older adults connected with their community, especially during times of social distancing.*

5. ***Participate in Lifelong Learning:*** *Many communities offer classes and workshops for older adults, ranging from art and music to technology and health. These programs provide opportunities to learn new skills, meet people with similar interests, and stay mentally active.*

https://wesleysecurecare.org/the-importance-of-community-for-older-adults/

SUGGESTIONS:

To help them feel valued, create a cookbook together, featuring their favorite recipes, and publish it. Presenting them with ideas and providing the freedom to be creative will affirm their existence.

Take them on outings, such as sightseeing or shopping trips to the shopping malls, strolls in the park, interactions with other people, or cooking their favorite meals while chatting in the kitchen. It's important to show them that they are loved and not forgotten.

Scientifically, you can retrain the minds of the elderly by teaching them to play brain-teasing games on their phones. Memory games help the elderly enhance their memory and cognitive abilities. They also increase focus, making them feel sharper.

Another suggestion is to create a workable visitation schedule so they can have frequent visitors. The mind can play tricks on the elderly, making them feel no longer needed, loved, or wanted. Finally, send videos to watch in their spare time, call or text, and send family photos. Better yet, take family photos together as they age—not only for them but for memories that will last a lifetime.

My Entire Body Belongs to Me! And I Will Always Protect Myself!

Take care of our elderly and disabled community, they deserve it!

A Simple Prayer

God of heaven, I know you alone can free my mind like a jaybird that flies untroubled in the summertime.

Lord, will you make my path clearer and more precise as I walk closer and closer to you?

Keep me safe morning, noon, and night as I travel to and fro, meeting people I have never met before.

Father, I need my confidence to flow as boldly as it once did; otherwise, nothing else will matter to me. Restore my joy, peace, and solitude as I walk freely in summer, spring, winter, and fall.

Thank You for helping me rise above the ashes, triumph over the path that sought to keep me in bondage, take a leap of faith, and experience all the delight life can offer.

—Dr. Sandra E. Jackson

Allow God to keep you in perfect peace!

To protect yourself, since you can't be sure who to trust with your vital information, you choose to keep it private. This secrecy can result in behavioral disorders and physical changes, such as acting out, disobeying your caring parents, and altering your appearance and personality.

Some people become promiscuous, and others exhibit loud and wild behavior, wearing and doing things outside their natural norm. Yet they maintain their calm demeanor as if nothing has ever happened. Still, they are masking their inner tormented soul.

Eventually, the truth will emerge, and the victim will either be re-victimized or supported.

If a child reports the perpetrator to the wrong person, they may be victimized again—blamed, dismissed as a liar, or ignored entirely. If the adult they confide in believes them but mishandles the critical information, it could lead to serious consequences, even violence.

If the adult handles it correctly, they will go to the city or state authorities and report it legally. Consequently, getting family members involved could lead to someone getting locked up, killed, or badly abused due to their initial reaction, emotional outburst, or retaliation.

Telling the correct person is key! Sharing what has occurred may be difficult; you may feel uncomfortable, withdrawn, or ashamed. Talk to the authorities at school, the police, or an attorney. It can be your teacher, pastor, coach, parent, or any person of authority. They will know what to do and who to contact.

Do not be afraid to share your pain; it is the first step of your healing journey.

Healing happens between the pages so keep reading.

It is a tactic to make you feel like you are all alone on your journey.

You have the power to say, "NO!"

Even though the shadows whisper

and doubts grip the soul,

you can still say, "NO!"

A chilling wave of unwanted fear

may rush into your already perfectly scripted story;

and although questions may appear,

go ahead and boldly speak up by shouting,

"NO!"

My Entire Body Belongs to Me! And I Will Always Protect Myself!

If you are confronted with unsolicited dangers,
slick and unnoticed advances that come toward you
with lurking threats, seeking to disrupt your peace,
you must hear a resounding cry that remains unheard
Yet, surfaces just in time to take back your peace, it
says Hey! Deep inside you lies the right to say, "NO!"

Thank God for the calm strength that emerges,
And the familiar voice that comes to guide you with care,
whispering, "Trust yourself;
my light is presently guiding you to safety
Know that the power above has your back."

Confidence and doubt may sway back and forth in your mind,
excitedly, confidence blooms with a steady hand,
navigating what could have been a tragedy,
into a beautiful true story of triumphant victory.

You embrace the peace with a sigh of joy,
realizing you have escaped sorrow, depression, and sadness,
because you trusted in yourself and listened to your inner voice
that demanded you to stand up in the moment and say,
'NO!'

Sandra E. Jackson

Your perpetrator could be anyone dressed in a tailored suit or a homeless person on the street. Parent, sibling, uncle, guest, auntie, niece, nephew, cousin or distant relative, teacher, preacher, pastor, clergy, secretary, friend, close neighbor or a neighbor down the street, visitor, co-worker, coach, boss, friend, significant other, husband, wife, college sweetheart, dorm roommate, a passenger on a bus, a driver, or a stranger, both male or female, child, or BFF may put you in danger.

Regardless of who it may be, you still have the power to protect your body by verbally saying, "NO!" and realizing that your body and all its parts belong to you 24/7, not them!

My "No!" is powerful

Hey! What does my/your "NO!" really mean? It means I know exactly who I am. I know my value and worth and refuse to let anyone sabotage my blissful, blessed future. My dreams will not be abolished; my destiny shall come to fruition, and nothing—not a single thing or person—will get in my way. My "No!" signifies that I recognize my life is a treasure; this is why the enemy is trying with all its might to sabotage my destiny. However, God has allowed me to see my bright future. Therefore, I will labor in prayer, fasting, and sacrifice as I fight to win, and no challenge can undermine what God has in store for me or you.

The most valuable relationship I have is with myself. Therefore, I refuse to abandon myself to please someone else, which leads to emptiness and chaos within. My "No" represents growth, peace, and contentment; yours can too. It is a vital tool that allows us to reclaim our time and personal space, while also reducing stress, anxiety, and other common emotions. My "No" enables me to focus on what truly matters inside. My "No" signifies that I have figured out who I am and that I have set clear boundaries that I refuse to ignore because my commitment to myself fosters balance and a fulfilling, abundant life. I will adhere to my "No" without succumbing to outside pressure, regardless of my opposition. My "No" is now a natural response, and I feel empowered.

Nobody else may defend you, so stand up and advocate for yourself.

"My Protector's Decree"

I assert that my entire being is inherently mine; I recognize the invaluable nature of this gift. It is imperative that I consistently safeguard my God-given treasure from

My Entire Body Belongs to Me! And I Will Always Protect Myself!

inappropriate advances, insidious whispers, and secrets that may compel me to retreat into myself.

Should an individual violate my boundaries, I understand that this transgression does not reflect my worth and will not define me. However, such actions may induce discomfort, invoking a visceral reaction within me and an overwhelming response that may be difficult to comprehend.

These encounters may engender debilitating fear and self-doubt that hinders my mental and emotional well-being, driving me to cry out emphatically, "NO!" as I hastily withdraw from the situation.

Yet, I ponder, where shall I seek refuge? Who can I confide in?

I will seek sanctuary in a place of tranquility, confiding in a trusted guardian or a compassionate educator who will lend an empathetic ear without judgment or reproach, who will not impose feelings of guilt or embarrassment, but I will strive to heal my wounds and alleviate my isolation pain.

I possess courage and acknowledge my inner strength.

Nonetheless, I recognize the need to address the injustices I have faced; injustices that deepen my desire for fairness, equity, and harmony. I remain hopeful for brighter days, where safety is within reach—days filled with clear blue skies, sparkling stars, and guiding lights that will lead me to my peaceful, newfound path of reality.

My Entire Body Belongs to Me! And I Will Always Protect Myself!

We have a mandate to protect our children. Secret Touches Are Always Bad:

Acknowledge any time someone touches you and tells you to keep it a secret; it is a deliberate act of wrongdoing. They are fully aware of the lifelong infraction they have caused you. To escape accountability, they resort to threats, vowing to harm your parents, family, or you if you don't speak out.

They will have leverage over you to control you for long periods of your life. Take back your power. This tactic typically works for the perpetrator because it embeds deep fear in the victim, allowing them to return without fear of being reported.

What will you do? You have options! But you must be bold and fearless, realizing you have nothing to lose. What can you do? Report the person and the behavior as soon as possible. To whom? To the highest authorities in whatever setting the incident occurred. If you are in school, the principal, guidance office, nurse's office, or a teacher will support you. You can reach out to the senior pastor if you are in church.

However, if it involves the senior pastor, you should find a trusted leader you feel comfortable confiding in, such as a police officer, parent, or clergy member. You must locate someone in charge, like an assistant, if they are unreachable. It is in your best interest never to leave without reporting the incident.

Secrets Are Toxic

- It is never all right to hold a secret of abuse. Secrets about touching are never okay.
- It is usually a "bad" touch if someone tells you to keep a secret about touching.
- Covering up wrong is wrong.
- Isolating yourself may lead to an unproductive life, alone.
- It takes grit, inner strength, and hope to move past the devastation.

Healing happens between the pages so keep reading.

Don't isolate yourself from society instead of healing.
Deal with IT!

Grief, regret, loss, guilt, pain, hurt, abuse, and devastation confuse the heart, gripping it tightly without any intention of releasing their hold. We often choose the less-traveled path, allowing us to ignore all this pain. However, that route is a winding country road that stretches on without an exit in sight.

Therefore, the healing process should quickly become a priority. It may take some time, but you are worth the effort and investment.

CHAPTER 3

Trust Your Instincts!

If something feels off, it is. Do not ignore your gut feeling. One of the worst things you can do to forfeit your life is not to trust your instincts. Suppose someone does something out of the ordinary. In that case, it is not your fault, so do not justify their actions, make excuses, or make up some preposterous story that they made a mistake or did not do what you know they did because you respect or look up to them.

They may have a prominent social position at church, workplace, or home. It is never an option for you to say, I do not want to disturb their life, marriage, children's lives, job, status, or the community. They have destroyed your life, focus, and the probability of progressing in forward motion; therefore, it is your obligation to now take the next step into your own hands. You are now getting retribution so that you can exist and THRIVE!

To ensure your safety, create enough space between you and

others, whether at the table where they can't put their feet on yours, or if they are on the playground, where they can't touch your private parts, or even in an automobile where they can't take advantage because they know you will be too embarrassed to scream.

The perpetrator knows, plots, and plans a perfect execution. It is strategic and meant to take you off-guard.

They may even lure you into an isolated room or level of the house where no one can hear or see. You must be constantly alert. You must step backward if they are too close. Why? To create enough distance between each of you. If they are on the phone, you must stipulate that they have crossed boundaries; if they continue, you must hang up quickly. If they are in a large crowd and it is difficult for you to escape, you must find a way to avoid danger. It is perfectly fine to do it scared!

Do not allow the crowd to intimidate you! Scream for HELP!

My Entire Body Belongs to Me! And I Will Always Protect Myself!

Clearly and firmly state, "Please give me some space," or "I'm uncomfortable with this." Make clear statements using the language you use. Why? Most people take it for granted that their approaches are welcomed, so to them, your "No!" does not mean "No!" Make eye contact with them. Use your emotions and facial expressions to express your "No!" Ensure there is no misunderstanding about your expression and that they get it!

Your eyes are the window to the soul; therefore, when you make direct eye contact, it will resonate with them that you mean what you have said. Tell them to stop. Sometimes, telling them to stop may not be enough. Go as far as you must go to maintain your innocence. After you say NO! Enforce your NO! Embrace your NO! And celebrate your NO!

Although someone touches you, you are the one who is obligated to act without delay. Every part of your body is off-limits to others, and you owe them nothing. Do not apologize to them for anything, and do not blame yourself for what they have done or tried to do. You can defend yourself unapologetically since they crossed the line by touching you.

Do not go into a shell.

You must go into a fight-or-flight reaction.

Say "No!" boldly!

You are worth IT!

Verbally, let your mouth move and your voice speak the words with authority: "No!" Repeat it as often as needed, and don't let anyone silence you! Yell, "HELP!" "STOP!" Push, scratch, bite, and run. Do whatever it takes to defend yourself, your body, mind, legacy, and your LIFE—because your peace is essential.

CHAPTER 4

Secrets? No Secrets Here!

Move away from the perpetrator as quickly as possible. Make sure you are in a safe place quickly. Do not hesitate to remove yourself from their presence and ensure you are unreachable on your cell phone, address, email, text, home phone, family members' home, etc.

- Look directly at the person and maintain eye contact. This can be a powerful deterrent.

- If the behavior escalates, speak loudly and clearly. Yell "Stop!" or "Help!" to attract attention.

- Move toward other people. Position yourself near an exit or where others can see you if possible.

- Not reporting the incident is not an option. Your only thought must be to do so quickly.

- Do not allow anyone to intimidate or shame you into going

through with unwanted gestures.

- Isolation is one tactic used on victims.
- The perpetrator ensures the victim is isolated from people, phones, and communication.
- Open your mouth, write it on paper, text it, call the authorities, and meet with them to report all unconsented acts. Help is attainable and receptive.

Unapologetically, look them straight in the face and say, "NO!"

CHAPTER 5

When? Immediately

If possible, record conversations, keep text messages, and report the incidents to a trusted church official staff member, respected member, or security personnel.

- If you feel unsafe, report immediately and contact the police or a local support organization.
- Say, I can stand resolute, firm, and bold.
- I am strong enough to defend myself daily.
- Say, I will not hold secrets from anyone.
- Secrets are not welcome here.
- Threats are not accepted.
- Paralyzing fear may grip your heart, mind, and body, but don't surrender to fear; do it scared!

My Entire Body Belongs to Me! And I Will Always Protect Myself!

Protective Measures: Safety doesn't happen by accident.

♦ Invest in a self-defense keychain alarm, Apple Air Tag, and phone applications such as Life360.

♦ Pepper spray, security door jammer, or security cameras.

♦ Educate yourself with self-defense videos available on the internet or YouTube.

♦ Stay alert at all times, looking from left to right and front to back, ensuring your safety in public.

If it happens on the bus, report it on the bus!

School Bus Driver Gets 95 to Life for Sex Assaults on 2 Girls

"A 43-year-old former school bus driver in Santa Ana was sentenced Wednesday to 95 years to life in prison for sexually assaulting two young girls he lived with, starting when they were about 6 and 8 years old.

Nery Rodriguez Gonzalez was convicted Sept. 18 of one count of continuous sexual abuse of a child and single counts each of lewd or lascivious acts with a minor younger than 14, aggravated sexual assault of a child younger than 14, aggravated sexual assault of a child with a foreign object and lewd or lascivious acts with a minor, all felonies.

"The sexual assaults continued for about four years, police said."

When he was charged in 2021, police said the defendant was working for Durham School Services and was driving a bus serving the Santa Ana Unified School District. But he was not charged with molesting any students.

Police were called to the children's hospital in Orange County on Dec. 30, 2020, when one of the girls told her mother the defendant had sexually abused her from when she was 8 until she was 13, police testified during a preliminary hearing. The molestation occurred in Santa Ana and Garden Grove, police testified.

One night while spending the night at the defendant's home with 3 siblings, one of the victims woke up to seeing Gonzalez having sex with another victim, police testified. That victim reported he had molested her starting when she was 6 or 7 until she was 13, police testified."

CHAPTER 6

Quotes For Teenagers

- "If you don't believe in yourself, why is anyone else going to believe in you." — Tom Brady

- "The only person you should try to be better than is the person you were yesterday." — Matty Mullins

- "Dear Teen, Love yourself. Forgive yourself. Be true to yourself. Because how you treat yourself sets the standard for how others treat you." — Steve Maraboli

- "Never apologize for being sensitive or emotional. Let this be a sign that you have a big heart and are not afraid to let others see it. Showing your emotions is a sign of strength." — Brigitte Nicole

- "You need to remember that love does not mean one person gives all and another person receives all." —Abirami P. Kurukkal

- "Never bend your head. Always hold it high. Look the world

straight in the eye."— Hellen Keller

♦ "Always admit when you're wrong. You will save thousands in therapy... and a few friendships too."— Harvey Fierstein

♦ "If you are always trying to be normal, you'll never know how amazing you can be." —Maya Angelou

As you take risks, remember that getting back up is all right!

Inspirational Quotes for Teenagers

♦ Sometimes, during the teen years, we just need a little reminder about going toward the good.

♦ "Beautiful people are not always good, but good people are always beautiful." —Imam Ali

♦ "You have to be authentic; you have to be true, and you

have to believe in your heart." —Howard Schultz

♦ "Always be a first-rate version of yourself, instead of a second-rate version of someone else." —Judy Garland

♦ "It takes courage to grow up and become who you really are." — E. E Cummings

♦ "The people who are crazy enough to think that they can change the world are the ones who do." —Steve Jobs

♦ "You must always have faith in people. And most importantly, you must always have faith in yourself." —Elle Woods, *Legally Blonde*

♦ "Never dull your shine for somebody else." —Tyra Banks

♦ "You will always pass failure on your way to success." —Mickey Rooney

♦ "No matter what anybody tells you, words and ideas can change the world." —Robin Williams

♦ "Act as if what you do makes a difference. It does." —William James

Important Considerations

♦ Safety First: Your safety is paramount. If you feel threatened, do whatever it takes to get away.

♦ Do not Blame Yourself: You are not responsible for the actions of others.

♦ When safe, seek support: Talking to a trusted parent, friend, family member, therapist, or support group can help you process the experience.

My Entire Body Belongs to Me! And I Will Always Protect Myself!

This is what freedom looks like. This can be YOU!

Tell a trusted adult right away. This could be:

- Your mom or dad
- Another family member you trust
- A teacher
- A school counselor
- A doctor
- The police
- Pastor
- Therapist
- Clergy

My Entire Body Belongs to Me! And I Will Always Protect Myself!

If you cannot go face-to-face for your mental health, online works as well.

CHAPTER 7

It's Important To Remember

During this low time, you may feel alone. Do not buy into that false emotion. Consequently, you are not alone and are not the only person who has suffered greatly. Statistics estimate that in 1998 17.7 million American women had been victims of attempted or completed rapes. And males, 2.78 million men (about the population of Mississippi).

Because someone has just violated your body, space, or person, you tend to feel ugly, unworthy, dirty, like used goods, or lacking in value. However, that is a trick to silence your voice and keep you quiet.

It's Not Your Fault

This is not your fault. If you're not cautious, the blame game can quickly take hold. Let me emphasize: it is not your fault. Why is that? Because you didn't cross any boundaries, they did. You might think that it wouldn't have occurred if you hadn't been there, hadn't agreed to meet them, or had brought someone along. You might convince yourself that they didn't overstep, or that it's your fault due to how you dressed, or because you were aware of their feelings for you and, in your mind, led them on. Perhaps you even said something that encouraged their actions. No!

Someone who harms another must take full responsibility for their actions. If you did not permit them to touch you or make inappropriate comments, it is not your fault they chose to do so.

You are not alone. Someone—an adult or an authority figure can help you if you dare to share what happened. Make sure to provide all the details.

I dare to heal the hurt!

Confront your fears; people are here to help you navigate them.

What Can I Do to Heal the Hurt?

IT MAY BE NECESSARY: Find a great therapist who can help heal the hurt and restore you to a healthy path to healing.

THE NECESSITY OF SOUL SEARCHING: It is important to search your conscience and be truthful, knowing you are not to blame.

THE NECESSITY OF TALKING IT OUT: Be open to sharing your complete story! The details may be painful, but expressing them from your mind, heart, and emotions is essential.

Holding them in your mind blocks, stagnates, and hinders growth, promoting sickness and disease.

THE NECESSITY OF SEEKING GOD: God can heal your pain better than anyone else. He truly cares about your well-being. Reading the Bible will also provide comfort, healing, and wholeness. It will offer the balanced perspective needed in this situation. Many churches offer groups to connect you with peers facing similar challenges.

THE NECESSITY OF FORGIVING: Forgiveness is not just for the other person; instead, it acts as a cathartic release for your own growth. Releasing self-blame will assign responsibility where it rightly belongs and allow you to move forward healthily.

THE NECESSITY OF FORGETTING: The majority do not realize that remembering a horrible incident is like carrying a dead person around with you 24/7. You become weighted down when you decide to hold on to baggage of such magnitude. Your conversation is heavy, your friends cannot help you move forward, and soon they will drop off; your demeanor becomes heavy, anger sets in, and that darkness is what takes over your entire life. You are better than that. Your future is at stake; therefore, you must decide to let it GO!

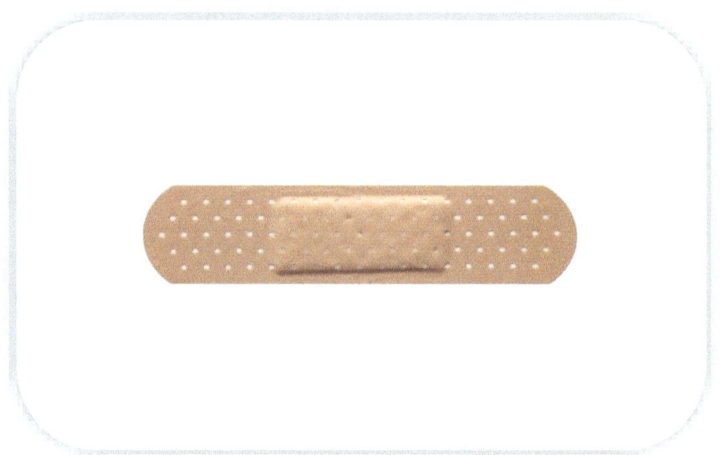

You may need a bandage now, but soon you will get better!

The Necessity of Your "No!"

You can say "NO!" to any inappropriate or unwelcome touch, and it will be all right. Touches that make you feel uncomfortable are wrong. Act quickly and state that you disagree with them. It is okay to talk about your body. You are in control of your body, and it is perfectly normal to talk about it without anyone crossing the line.

**Healing happens between the pages,
so keep reading.**

My Entire Body Belongs to Me! And I Will Always Protect Myself!

It's your time to heal!

Remember These Few Important Rules

Your entire body is yours, so embrace it. Your fingers, toes, ears, and nose belong to whom? To you! Your eyes, ears, and even your unwanted tears belong to whom? To you! Your breasts, buttocks, private parts, shoulders, and neck all belong not to your neighbor, but to whom? Yes, to you! Therefore, whether you are young, middle-aged, or mature; petite, average-sized, or pleasantly plump; tall, short, or of smaller stature; unattractive, beautiful, or stunning, you have the right to protect every layer, every part, and every imprint of your God-given form, which belongs solely to whom? YOU!

My Entire Body Belongs to Me! And I Will Always Protect Myself!

You are not alone, and there are trained professionals to help you.

CHAPTER 8

Affirmations About Body Safety

These daily affirmations can be repeated whenever you feel anxious, nervous, or uncertain. Following these guidelines can strengthen your confidence and empower children to protect themselves.

- Say, "I am necessary. I have been sent here to make a difference in the world." (Benefits: Builds confidence and awareness)

- "I am protected. I am treasured. I am strong." (Benefits: Provides safety and self-worth)

- "My entire body is mine. I have the right to say no to any touch that makes me feel uncomfortable." (Benefits: Provides independence and body autonomy with the right to set boundaries)

My Entire Body Belongs to Me! And I Will Always Protect Myself!

♦ "It is okay to talk about my body and how I feel." (Benefits: Encourages openness about sensitive topics)

♦ "I trust my automatic instincts. If something feels dishonest, I will speak up." (Benefits: Promotes awareness and the necessity of trusting one's gut feelings)

♦ "I am never alone. There are several people I can trust to help me." (Benefits: Reassures children that they will always have a support system)

♦ "I can protect myself and face my fears." (Benefits: instills a sense of confidence and self-empowerment)

♦ "I will ensure my safety and happiness." (Benefits: Provides a sense of hope and optimism for the person)

Do the right thing! Report the details, even if you are afraid.

CHAPTER 9

Remember: Knowledge Allows For Open Dialogue And Authentic Conversation

Unity:

♦   In the home, everyone must create a safe and open environment for communication.

♦   Everyone must use age-appropriate language.

♦   Every adult must listen to the child's concerns without judgment.

♦   Everyone must know that there are options to seek professional help if needed.

Open communication, education, and positive affirmations create a vibrant, healthy, and supportive environment. This understanding can aid children in establishing healthy boundaries and building strong self-worth.

All adults responsible for children's well-being and safety must maintain a secure environment in the school bus, locker room, lunchroom, storage areas, camp, hotel, church, vehicle, restroom, playground, and other places where children may be.

Keep a support system, someone who will listen without blame.

Parents, Children Grow Up!

When children grow up, they will need therapy, counseling, and mentorship if they have been abused and taken advantage of. When a child is abused, their emotions and hormones are no longer aligned, which causes anger issues that can spiral their lives out of control. The jails are filled with grown adults who were once children who were not handled correctly. Consequently, I wrote this book as a guide to equip children with the knowledge they need to protect themselves, even when an adult is not around.

- Teaching children that they are enough is crucial.
- Self-Esteem: Parents, consider whether your child has high

or low self-esteem.

♦ Understanding your child's demeanor, personality, likes, and dislikes is vital.

♦ Leaving babies alone is unacceptable, whether at home, in the car, or at neighbors' houses.

♦ Leaving children alone for long periods is unhealthy.

♦ Daily communication and open dialogue are important.

♦ Children must know they can freely talk and share their thoughts and feelings with adults without fear of judgment, backlash, or trouble.

♦ Encourage your child to look in the mirror and say, "I love you." If they struggle with this, it could indicate low self-esteem. Knowledge is power; recognizing this early gives parents an advantage, allowing them to seek the necessary support for their child.

See yourself the way God sees you! You are beautiful!

CHAPTER 10

Remember That You Are Loved

Your safety is the top priority. You must remain safe at all times. Although challenging, safety must be at the forefront of your mind whenever you plan or make arrangements with anyone, accept an engagement, party invite, play date, or luncheon with family, friends, colleagues, co-workers, or clergy, or examine the location to ensure a safe environment.

Firmness and an unshaken or indifferent attitude is also necessary. Each requires mental strength to stand up for what is right. Saying "No!" is one thing, but genuinely meaning it, enforcing it, and standing firm in it is an entirely different challenge. You have people who adore and care about your well-being, and you must realize this when things are complicated and when they are not—knowing that you are loved and cared for changes the picture altogether.

The difference between someone who knows, guesses, or supposes and those who feel they have no one to advocate for them is enormous. Family support goes a long way. When the bond is strong, you never have to second-guess whom you can confide in—maintaining relationships with the heads of families and business owners, such as your school, college, coach, or librarian.

Remembering that you are loved is crucial for moving forward healthily.

Important to Note

Parents are encouraged to engage in open and ongoing discussions with their children about body safety. It is suggested that you use the information in this book as a foundational resource for tackling complex topics within homes, libraries, workplaces, educational institutions, childcare facilities, places of worship, and other domestic settings.

Healing happens between the pages, so keep reading.

Your family cares deeply for you and genuinely wants you to be happy.

We must create an open dialogue and an atmosphere where everyone feels safe, and their discussion is considered worthy and valid. When people reveal the truth, they will not have any worries about their safety, no matter who is involved.

Eliminating safety concerns will promote a quicker healing process. If an individual has excessive worries and perceives a lack of belief or trust from others, they may become anxious, withhold information, and distance themselves to protect against potential embarrassment, backlash, blame, or anxiety arising from their acceptance situation.

Reminder:

- Use age-appropriate language.
- Be patient and understanding.
- Listen to your child's concerns without interruption or bias.
- Seek professional, pastoral, or parental help if needed.

Protecting children, teenagers, adults, grandparents, and parents is essential! This book's primary goal is to educate parents, children, teenagers, and adults that their bodies belong solely to them, and that they have the right to protect themselves from unwanted touching, violations, or sexual advances.

Dinner time is a suitable time to check in with the entire family.

CHAPTER 11

One's Body's Autonomy

- Explain that their body is their own and that they can decide who touches them and how.
- Use age-appropriate language to discuss distinct types of touch. Example: Hugs, handshakes, and pats are how some touches can feel uncomfortable or wrong.
- Emphasize that no one, regardless of their relationship with the child, has the right to touch them in a way that makes them feel uncomfortable or scared.
- Identifying safe and unsafe touches.
- Teach children the difference between "good touches" (hugs from loved ones, high fives) and "bad touches" (any touch that makes them feel uncomfortable, scared, or confused).
- Explain that "bad touches" can come from anyone, even people they know and trust.
- Using their voice is imperative.

My Entire Body Belongs to Me! And I Will Always Protect Myself!

♦   Teach children to use their voice to say "NO!" firmly and loudly if someone tries to touch them inappropriately.

♦   Please encourage them to leave the situation immediately and tell a trusted adult.

♦   Reassure the person that they will have support when they report an incident.

♦   Create an atmosphere conducive to open communication.

♦   There must be an open and trusting environment where children and adults feel comfortable discussing their concerns about their bodies or safety.

♦   Create a schedule for regular check-ins to ask if they have questions or concerns.

♦   Provide distinct types of up-to-date safety resources.

♦   Ensure that up-to-date, age-appropriate resources are not limited to helpful information.

Find someone you trust, feel safe with, and can confide in.

- Child safety classes, therapists, counselors, and heads of child facilities are a few resources to look up.
- You can tell a parent, teacher, or other family member about what happened.

Important Information:

We provide guidelines to ignite your interest and help you identify the right services for you and your family. Each person will have unique needs based on their stage, age, or developmental level. Keep in mind that no one's situation is exactly the same, and that's perfectly fine; everyone's needs can vary.

Create an atmosphere conducive to open communication

CHAPTER 12

Teaching Parental Moments

- Remember, you won't be with your child 24/7, so prepare them for the real world.
- Teach them that their body is a precious being (the Temple of the Holy Spirit).
- Teach them in a fun way, using games, questions, and literature to help them stay safe.
- Research different guides on body safety (library database).
- It is essential to empower children to say "NO!" and show them how to react to unsafe situations.
- Your child trusts your judgment and the people you allow into their space.
- Be mindful of your actions and interactions.
- You will feel lost at times.
- You will feel like it won't get better, but it will.
- Never think or speak negatively about your child.

My Entire Body Belongs to Me! And I Will Always Protect Myself!

- You will need a strong, supportive team.
- You can't do it alone; you are not an island.
- You are loved.
- People may judge you, but don't allow that to stop you.
- Your child may say they hate you, but they do not mean it.
- They are searching for help—don't take it personal.

Intriguing and Engaging Messages

- Discovering the secrets to keeping your body happy and healthy will empower you.
- Learn to accept the journey of self-discovery, learn about your body, and protect it.
- Your body is your most valuable asset, so investing in keeping it safe is essential.
- Unveiling the power of "NO!" and building a world where every child knows they can be safe.

Holding hands builds confidence and security!

Direct and Informative Guidelines

♦ Parents, when your child comes to you to confide in you, please listen without judgment and blame. They are afraid and do not know what to do with their bodies and emotions. Their hormones have shifted, and it is unclear who is at fault or what next steps to take, if any.

♦ Parents do not become overwhelmed with guilt.

♦ Do not blame yourself if it is not your fault.

♦ If it is your fault, please apologize and get the necessary help via counseling, your local church, or a licensed professional.

♦ Express your sincere love.

Parents Create A Forever Bond With The Entire Family

♦ Do not be afraid to show your vulnerability. Children need to know they are always in a safe place.

- It is all right for you to cry together.

- Show affection if it is allowed.

- Be sensitive to your children's emotions.

- Parents, do not be afraid to deal with the new reality; healing is a process that may take longer than expected. Do not rush the process. Sometimes, the pain and hurt will fluctuate.

- Your child did not ask for the hurt and pain; therefore, we must navigate them to wholeness.

- Make sure you communicate openly with your child by interacting with them regularly so that if anything ever happens, they will feel comfortable coming and disclosing every detail with you.

- Having one-on-one time with each child lets them experience your love individually.

- A strong, supportive bond will make them feel a part of the family unit.

- They will understand that whatever happens to them also happens to the family.

- Having a support system before anything happens will equip them for any mishaps.

- Expressing daily connections of love empowers them to protect themselves daily.

- Know when to hold them and know when to fold them.

- If a child is unwilling to speak with you, give them space. (Within reason.)

- If they say it is too stressful, take a break.
- Be discerning, alert, and concerned. (Make sure they can feel your love.)
- Recognize changes in your child's behavior.

The entire family is involved with your future

- If a child calls you names, lashes out at you, or says something hurtful, know that they are hurting badly, which is called displaced anger.
- Know that the person closest to them is the one who feels the wrath of their hurt. It does not mean they hate or dislike you; it means they are confused, hurt, and angry. They do not know what to do or how to feel.
- Pay close attention to the age-appropriate conversations and the age of each talk.

- Protect young children from advanced information and keep them mentally safe, as they cannot unlearn something once it is spoken about.
- Always keep your child's mental health in mind.
- When a child feels violated, remember it is not about you. It is only about them.

Training a child is essential. Only provide age-appropriate information.

- Please do not allow your pride or emotions to prevent them from healing by disbelieving the details of their story.
- Do not allow others, such as family members or the community, to hinder your mindset and the process of getting your child the needed help.
- Do not be afraid to press charges or report what has

transpired.

- Hold your child and provide emotional support in the moment.
- Parents, I encourage you also to find a support system for yourself.
- Look in the Yellow Pages, or social media groups for like-minded people.
- Do not expect the same treatment for everyone. Each situation is different.
- Never say, "Get over it!"
- Never condemn your child or yourself.
- Prove to be trustworthy. Even when you want to doubt them, do not.
- Remember, they can feel whether you are on their side.
- Pray with them.
- Let them know you are always available.
- Be present.
- Let them know you do not have all the answers, but you will work together to achieve a healing state of mind.
- Depression is real. Try to prevent them from going into deep depression.
- They have medication that can suppress the pain.
- Walk the journey with your child. It may take years; be faithful.

My Entire Body Belongs to Me! And I Will Always Protect Myself!

Everyone's journey is different, so listen to and support them on their level.

♦   Parents may be unable to afford the help, but some organizations will support them financially.

♦   Do not allow embarrassment or pressure from others to hinder you from getting help.

♦   Your life belongs to you, so do exactly what is best for your well-being.

♦   You're never too wealthy to receive the needed help/support.

♦   You're never too poor to get the necessary assistance.

My Entire Body Belongs to Me! And I Will Always Protect Myself!

Protect and guard your peace; laughter, freedom, and liberty are yours.

♦ You're not too entitled to get assistance.

♦ Please do not allow anyone to judge you because it will stop you from healing and moving forward.

♦ Give yourself the power to take your life into your own hands.

♦ Be bold and unapologetic; your life is yours.

♦ Ask questions!

♦ You're smart, intellectual, and worthy of your innocence.

♦ You can do it! You did not do anything wrong.

♦ It is all right!

♦ You're enough.

Regardless of your status or economic condition, you can heal, too!

♦ Educate children regarding body safety in an engaging and age-appropriate manner.

♦ At each developmental stage, it is imperative that your child feels empowered with essential tools presented in a nurturing and enjoyable format.

♦ The learning process is most effective when free from stress.

♦ Provide guidance and resources in an enjoyable and age-appropriate fashion.

♦ Encourage children to understand that it is acceptable to voice their concerns and seek assistance.

♦ Each child can acquire the confidence necessary to articulate their needs and solicit support.

My Entire Body Belongs to Me! And I Will Always Protect Myself!

Healing happens between the pages, so keep reading.

Teenagers love your parents, and like in the Monopoly game, give them a "get out of jail free" card.

Parents, love your children unconditionally and give them a "get out of jail free" card.

Everyone faces difficult situations, and sticking together is key. Remember, recovery is possible.

We are stronger together.

My Entire Body Belongs to Me! And I Will Always Protect Myself!

The possibilities are endless when you do the work.
Say, "NO!"

CHAPTER 13

Believe That Healing Is Attainable For You!

If you have been abused and have remained silent, now is your time to heal. Prioritize yourself today. Silence suffocates and erodes the inside of your body. Keeping secrets does not lead to wholeness; it is like cancer that gnaws at your core.

You are not prey.

You are off-limits to those who impose themselves on you.

It is cathartic to confront it.

It is no longer something to be embarrassed about.

It is healing!

Inhale and exhale.

You deserve wholeness!

Take action today.

I recommend you journal every detail in a notebook and title your story. Then, write down detail-for-detail from your vantage.

Your truth serves as a healer.

Warning: It's okay if tears fall; taking a break is perfectly fine! You might feel overwhelmed and wish to pause, too. However, that is not healthy. You must push through because your breakthrough awaits you after you complete your story.

True story

While working at a facility in the early morning for a few hours, I received a call on my phone. On the other end was a person in tears. They began to share details of a nonconsensual encounter. It left them paralyzed, devastated, broken, and emotionally adrift. Physically, it was the worst night and early morning of their lives.

God spoke to my inner being, and I asked, "Do you have a pen and a piece of paper?" The reply was yes. I told them to trust the process, start writing down what happened to them in detail, and understand that I am here with them.

As the process continued, they cried and wept, saying, "I need to stop," and then, "All right, I'm back and ready to finish."

Since they dealt with their pain and pressed charges, they are now married, with children, and living the good life.

**Let your tears flow—they are cathartic!
They release trauma.**

You can be free as well! What does freedom look like for you? Your future looks bright and fulfilling, and we are waiting for you to embrace it. However, you must first believe it is possible and that you deserve a better life.

Do you have faith in the size of a grain of mustard seed? It is the tiniest seed on the market, and you can cover significant territory with just a little faith.

As your faith increases, it will place you before the correct people who will align with you on your road to recovery.

What is faith? The blending of trust and action all in one.

My Entire Body Belongs to Me! And I Will Always Protect Myself!

**Your future is bright!
Get Free and liberated today!**

ABOUT THE AUTHOR

Sandra E. Jackson is a Shiftologist, and the 12th child of the late Bishop Samuel I. Rumph and Elect Lady Priscilla M. Rumph. Sandra's preferred genre is inspirational, uplifting, and transformational for the mindset.

She is a National and International #1 bestselling author, a life insurance agent, an inspirational ordained evangelist, and much more. She is a member of the Honors Society, received the ACHI award, and has been featured in articles and on the cover of magazines. However, her most outstanding achievement is giving birth to her 9 adorable children.

Sandra is the visionary behind three anthologies: *Life After... Raising Children Wasn't Easy, But It Is Worth It!* and *The Cancer Experience: Nine True Stories.* You can explore her solo projects on the store page of her website and leave her a review.

Regarding achieving personal goals, Sandra is the #1 evening host of Sandra's Authors Forum Talk Show, which airs Thursdays at 8 PM EST on the Stellar Award-nominated Awesome God Radio. One of Sandra's most cherished memories was the evening before her 73rd birthday when she had the extraordinary opportunity to interview the incomparable motivational speaker Dr. Les Brown. He affirmed that she motivated the motivator!

When graduation seemed impossible, she persevered through life's unexpected challenges, including cancer. On May 29, 2021, she graduated from Nazarene Bible College with her bachelor's degree in theology and biblical studies. Following this, Sandra walked across the stage at Morehouse College in Atlanta, Georgia, to receive her Humanitarian Doctorate Degree in June 2024 in the Dr. Martin Luther King Jr. Auditorium for her remarkable contributions to society.

Sandra went through a divorce after more than 21 years of marriage, which changed her life. Consequently, she has focused on advocating for single mothers with children. Her nonprofit, Journey Into Purpose Development Foundation INC., is set to launch by 2027.

She lives by the mantra, "Just Get It Done!" Her favorite quote is, "I am ecstatic to be ALIVE!" You have the power to say, "No!"

Ways to connect with Dr. Sandra E. Jackson

Website: https://journeyintopurposellc.com/

Review: https://journeyintopurposellc.com/reviews/

X: https://twitter.com/EcstaticSandra

Twitch: https://www.twitch.tv/sandraspoetryspot

Ecstatic Calendar: https://calendly.com/ecstaticcoaching

Donate: https://journeyintopurposellc.com/donate/

Enter prepared with confidence and wisdom.

DEDICATION

This book is dedicated to all children, especially those who have experienced sexual abuse.

Know that you are not alone.

You are brave.

You are strong.

You are resilient.

You are loved.

Healing is possible right now.

Although a parent's mandate is to ensure their child's safety, they are not with their children 24/7. Therefore, this book will empower and educate children with the boldness, awareness, and authority to always look out for themselves. This book is dedicated to children in foster care, daycares, schools, parks, and homes. Children and adults must know they can keep and maintain their personal space joyfully and confidently. I aim to provide courage to the children who have survived sexual abuse and offer a message of hope and healing.

REFERENCES

https://parentingteensandtweens.com/inspirational-quotes-for-teenagers/

https://people.com/elementary-school-staffer-accused-waking-boy-sleepover-sexually-assault-8741754

https://rainn.org/statistics/children-and-teens

https://www.istockphoto.com/en/search/2/image?alloweduse=availableforalluses&mediatype=photography&phrase=police%20copenhagen&phraseprocessing=excludenaturallanguage

https://www.msn.com/en-us/news/crime/ohio-man-sexually-assaulted-and-filmed-toddlers-at-in-home-daycare/ar-AA1yltOL

https://www.msn.com/en-us/news/crime/school-bus-driver-gets-95-to-life-for-sex-assaults-on-2-girls/ar-AA1u3cqG

https://www.ourmental.health/mind-body-connection/the-power-of-touch-how-oxytocin-strengthens-bonds-and-boosts-well-being

https://www.psychologytoday.com/us/blog/protecting-children-from-sexual-abuse/202105/the-long-lasting-consequences-of-child-sexual

https://www.reptileknowledge.com/reptile-pedia/when-red-touches-black.

https://www.yourtango.com/2017307474/inspirational-quotes-sexual-assault-victim-shaming

All Photos: Free Stock Images

My Entire Body Belongs to Me! And I Will Always Protect Myself!

Your safety is important!

Stick together and protect each other!

The End

Disclaimer

This information is intended solely for general guidance and should not be interpreted as legal or professional advice. Each facility must establish comprehensive policies and procedures to prevent and address harassment and abuse.

Sandra E. Jackson

www.ingramcontent.com/pod-product-compliance
Lightning Source LLC
Chambersburg PA
CBHW040458240426
43665CB00039B/79